The Making of
The
Hitch-Hiker
Illustrated

This is the story of a gun, a car,
a deranged spree killer,
a unique woman
movie director
and a film
that made

Noir History!

The Making of
The
Hitch-Hiker
Illustrated

**by
Mary Ann
Anderson**

BearManor Media

2013

The Making of *The Hitch-Hiker* Illustrated

© 2013 Mary Ann Anderson

Certificate of Registration
TXu 1-860-151

For information, address:

BearManor Media
P. O. Box 71426
Albany, GA 31708

bearmanormedia.com

Typesetting and layout by John Teehan

Published in the USA by BearManor Media

ISBN— 1-59393-759-8
978-1-59393-759-1

This book is dedicated to Ida Lupino for her courage to tackle the Motion Picture Association and the Federal Bureau of Prisons, thereby allowing her to write, direct and produce The Hitch-Hiker *which became a classic Film Noir.*

Bravo, Ida!

Table of Contents

Introduction

Why We Made
The Hitch-Hiker
by Collier Young
and Ida Lupino

(From the original promotion for the film)

ONCE IN A LONG WHILE life itself turns up story material more exciting, more real and urgent than fiction. Such material started us on *The Hitch-Hiker*.

But before we put it into production we asked ourselves:

Will it make a GOOD picture?

Will it make people want to see it?

Can it be exploited for extra box-office returns?

THE HITCH-HIKER provided a YES answer to all three questions.

The deeper we delved into the subject, the more excited we became. We were dealing with real people caught in one of the most dramatic adventures of our times. The basic theme was the question—In a race against death, which survives? The sane or the criminal mind? The answer provides the strange, driving sequence of THE HITCH-HIKER.

As we proceeded, daily newspaper headlines proved over and over again that we had drama and excitement and reality in our subject. They also convinced us that we had a film which would be effectively exploited by smart showmen everywhere.

1

Thanks to this and the brilliant starring performances by Edmond O'Brien, Frank Lovejoy and William Talman, we think you'll remember the 70 minutes of THE HITCH-HIKER for a long time!

I asked Ida Lupino how did this film production start?

"I had gone to Palm Springs to receive an award from The Foreign Press Association for Woman of the Year. While I was there in Palm Springs, I interviewed Forrest Damron, one of the two hunters who had been held prisoner by Billy Cook. I was captivated by his story and wanted to bring this story to the big screen.

'He put the .38 in my face and I told Jim you'd better look around. I think we are in grave danger. He ordered Jim to keep both hands on the wheel where he could see them and he told me to place my arms on the dash. He asked for our wallets, taking Jim's first and mine second. He took our money and kept Jim's identification cards and registration for the car. He told us he was going over to old Mexico, dispose of the car and remain there on the money, that from here he was Jim Burke, and if we didn't do as he said, he'd kill us and dump our bodies in the Gulf.'

– Forrest Damron to Ida Lupino

"When I returned from Palm Springs I had my company, Filmakers release a statement announcing our plans to make a picture based on the frightening experience of the kidnapped hunters."

– Ida Lupino.

FILMMAKERS' RELEASE STATEMENT:
The story comes to the screen right out of the newspaper headlines. With terrifying conviction it depicts the experience of two Americans when they are captured by a hitch-hiker murderer and held as hostage at gunpoint while he has them drive across Mexico to a gulf port so he can escape to Central America.

Their journey is fraught with terror as they try to outwit their captor, knowing he plans to kill them when they reach their destination. Suspense never slackens as they proceed on their weird journey through the picturesque Mexican wastelands. The climax will make any audience hold its breath.

In a 22-day crime spree crisscrossing from California to Texas and back again, Cook killed six people, an entire vacationing family in Oklahoma, and another kidnapped motorist in California. Taking hostages was how he navigated America's intercity road network, making the William E. Cook story adaptable to excite cinemagoers who knew the loneliness of the open road in *The Hitch-Hiker,* a Filmakers production for RKO Radio distribution.

The Story of William Edward Cook, Jr.

"I never had a friend in all my life!"

WILLIAM EDWARD COOK, JR., alias "Billy Boy" or "Cockeyed Cook," was born in a shack in Joplin, Missouri, on December 23, 1928. His mother, Lauren Stevens, died when he was five years old. One night, his father, after drinking in a tavern, hopped a freight train and left Billy and his other seven children—six girls and another boy—to survive alone in an abandoned mine with just a few supplies. The children were left to fend for themselves. They were later discovered by the authorities huddled in the mine and living like animals.

All the children were placed into foster care, except Billy. He was small in size and had a deformed right eye with a belligerent attitude. Billy showed early signs of violent psychopathic behavior. He threw temper tantrums. Billy was very demanding and had an uncontrollable temper.

These character traits stopped welfare workers from finding someone to adopt him. He became a ward of the State. Billy was placed in reform school, where he was described as neat and quiet with nice handwriting but could not control his temper. He was involved in many fights. Billy was eventually placed in the care of a woman who accepted State money to look after him. This woman only took Billy Cook in because she wanted the money. They had an unfortunate relationship and never got along. A bicycle was purchased for Billy but she did not want to make the payments so it was returned. On July 15, 1941 this foster mother returned him to the court. Other guardians found Billy to be uncontrollable.

As Billy got older, he would stay out late at night and get into trouble.

"*I never had a friend in all my life. Nobody ever liked me and they never will. Nobody ever did anything for me. They always did things to me.*"

"Billy Boy" drifted into petty crime and was eventually arrested for truancy. At the age of twelve, he told a judge he would prefer reformatory rather than more foster care.

"*They sent me to a reform school when I was eleven. There they beat me. They used a rubber hose and beat me all the time.*"

Cook had the words "*hard luck*" tattooed across the knuckles of both of his hands. Billy got his wish; he robbed a cab driver of $100.00 and stole a car. He was soon caught and sent back to reform school, spending the next five years in detention before he transferred at age seventeen to the Missouri State Penitentiary.

"*Then I went to the penitentiary. There was a bunch of dumb guards— they couldn't even read—beat me on the head every time they saw me. They called me "Cockeyed Cook." They were rough and mean, always mean as hell.*"

While in prison, Billy assaulted another inmate with a baseball bat, and this inmate almost died. Billy Cook became one of the most dangerous inmates in the prison.

When Billy Cook was released from prison, he returned to Joplin to be reunited only briefly with his father. Billy told his father it was his intention now "*to live by the gun and roam.*" He left for the small desert town of Blythe, California. There Billy worked as a dishwasher in a diner, saving up money to buy a gun. In late December, Billy Cook headed on for El Paso Texas. This time he did not travel alone—his new traveling companion was a snub-nosed .32 caliber pistol that he kept tucked away under his belt. Cook had no use for people, Billy hated everyone.

On December 28, 1950 Billy Cook launched his senseless killing spree and within seven days he had become a criminal legend. Billy reigned as the terror of the south western region of the United States. In a two-week period, Cook murdered six persons—including an entire family from Illinois—kidnapped three others and became the object of a nationwide manhunt.

Billy Cook's peak of criminal notoriety came when *Life* magazine, then essential reading in millions of households, ran five pages of photographs of him and the massacred victims. Cook had taken a place in criminal history next to Pretty Boy Floyd and John Dillinger.

Coverage by *Life* magazine, in the 1950s was the equivalent of an hour long special on every news broadcast and cable channels today. *Life*'s reporting was reinforced by banner headlines in the newspapers all over the country about the pursuit of Billy. It was so large a man hunt that it over shadowed anything in the John Dillinger and Pretty Boy Floyd era.

Texas mechanic Lee Archer, from Tahoka, Texas, was driving his car near Lubbock, Texas on the way to Oklahoma City when he picked up Billy Cook, who was hitch-hiking. Once inside the car Billy stated, *"Keep driving mister. I'm engineerin' this trip from here. We ain't stoppin' nowhere till I say so."* With an automatic pointed at his head, Archer drove through Oklahoma City. Cook ordered Archer to stop the car.

Cook robbed Archer of $85.00 at gun point, taking the money from the wallet he found in Archer's pocket. Billy forced him into the trunk of his car. Cook, unfamiliar with the manual transmission on the stolen black Buick convertible, took Archer on the ride of his life—fast, slow with jerking motions. Cook got the car stuck in a ditch on a hill. Archer pried opened the trunk lid with a screw driver. Cook could see Archer in the rear view mirror trying to get out of the trunk, so he slammed on the brakes. Archer opened the trunk and took off running. Cook got out of the car waving his gun, *"Come back you 'sonovabitch' or I'll kill you!"* Archer ran into the bushes and hid. He saw his Buick take off in a cloud of dust.

On a turn near Luther, the Buick stalled. Cook could not get it started, so he left the car. He flagged down a blue 1949 Chevrolet sedan.

Archer escaped with his life by walking on a small back road to town. He then called the Police.

By the time the Police arrived, Cook had taken off in the blue Chevy, heading west on U.S. Hwy 66. Inside Archer's car, the police found a duffel bag with clues to tie it to the hitchhiker. There were several T-shirts with the laundry mark initials "W. E. C.," and a box which had a new .32 Colt's automatic cleaning brush, along with a second box containing thirty-six rounds of ammunition with fourteen cartridges missing. A receipt for the purchase of the gun from an El Paso store, showing the guns serial number—made out to "W. E. Cook, St. Louis" was also discovered. Using newspaper wire photo machines, officials soon had pictures and the Missouri Penitentiary records of William E. Cook. He was 5 feet 6 inches tall, 145 pounds and tattooed. He had an eye that did not close due to an operation to remove a growth on the eye lid when he was a child.

Billy Cook's next targets would not be so lucky.

Cook had posed as a hitch-hiker again between Claremore and Tulsa Oklahoma. Farmer Carl Mosser, from Atwater, Illinois, along with his wife, Thelma, their three children, Ronald Dean (age 7), Gary Carl (age 5) and Pamela Sue (age 3) and their dog picked up Billy on their route to

Albuquerque, New Mexico. The Mossers were going to visit Mosser's twin brother Chris. Cook immediately took the family hostage at gun point. Billy forced Mosser to drive aimlessly for 72 hours.

Mosser nearly overpowered Cook when they stopped at Roy's Gas Station near Wichita Falls for some fuel. Mosser told Cornwell, the elderly attendant, to fill the tank. When he asked, at Cook's orders, for some lunch meat, the attendant told him he would have to get it himself.

They went inside the station. Mosser grabbed hold of Cook, but Billy was too strong for him. Mosser attempted to free his family, crying out, *"For God's sake help me! Help me! He's going to kill my wife and children!"* Cook swung Mosser against the wall, shattering a window. Mosser still had a weak hold on Cook. Cornwell's temper flared and he hopped behind the counter. The frightened old attendant pulled out a .44 caliber revolver and waved it at the struggling men. He ordered Mosser to let loose of Cook. Mosser tried to explain again what was happening. Cornwell threatened to shoot. Cook was now in charge again—his hand was in his pocket, where he kept his gun.

The scared attendant ordered both men out of the station.

Cook ordered Mosser back to the car. Cornwell followed them outside. He saw a woman in the car. Her face was full of terror. They sped away. Realizing he made a mistake, Cornwell had his friend Skinner, who was outside, get into his truck and chase them down the road. Cook saw him driving behind them and fired several shots at the attendant's friend. Skinner stopped and gave up the chase.

Cook was angry and ordered Mosser to drive to Carlsbad, New Mexico, then on to El Paso Texas, to Houston and then to Winthorp, Arkansas. After a 2,500 mile journey that started in Oklahoma, went through Wichita Falls, back to Houston and finally ending in Joplin, Missouri Billy had Mosser stop the car.

After 72 hours of being kidnapped, Thelma Mosser broke down in tears. The three children started crying as well. Cook gagged all of them except Mosser. Unfortunately, a police car was watching the Mosser Car. Billy Cook, as mentally unstable as he was, shot the entire Mosser Family, including their pet dog.

Cook grew more and more tired after he dumped the Mosser bodies in a mine shaft near Joplin, Missouri. Billy Cook then headed back to California after abandoning Mosser's car in Oklahoma.

The grimy blue 1949 Chevrolet car was later discovered by authorities on January 3, 1951, in a ditch 3 miles northwest of Tulsa, Oklahoma.

The car had a bullet punctured back seat—blood was everywhere, stained and torn blankets, children's clothes covered in blood, but there were no bodies to be found. Police were horrified when they found two "Hopalong Cassidy" hats in the empty car, a baseball glove, a doll, a woman's purse with a set of keys, $200 in traveler's checks, family photos and a driver's license with the name of Thelma Mosser.

Relatives of the Mosser Family had been expecting the Mosser's for several days and had not heard from them—they feared the worst.

Within hours on January 3, 1951, the largest manhunt in United States history, up to that time, had begun with 2,000 law enforcement officers joined by another 1,000 police, game wardens and private citizens. Despite an "All Points Bulletin," Cook was able to reach Blyth, California, by bus and hitchhiking, on January 6.

Outside Blythe, Sheriff Deputy Homer Waldrip had become suspicious of Billy Cook. Waldrip went to a motel room to question an acquaintance of Billy's. The Sheriff Deputy was taken by surprise when Cook himself jumped out from behind the door and took his revolver. The deputy was kidnapped at pistol point and taken hostage by the killer. Cook forced Waldrip to drive around aimlessly for forty miles in the desert, as he did with Carl Mosser.

Billy Cook bragged about killing the Mosser Family from Illinois. *"The kids were crying, the dame was hysterical and started screaming. It was too risky. I didn't want the cops on me, so I plugged them all!"*

Cook ordered the deputy to pull over the car. He forced Waldrip to get out of the cruiser and to lie face down in a ditch several miles from the main road. Billy tied him up with blanket strips. He told him he was going to shoot a bullet into the back of his head but he did not do this; instead Cook got into the Police car and sped away, leaving Deputy Waldrip to die.

The Sheriff Deputy got loose and walked to the main road, where he was picked up several hours later and driven back to town. Waldrip had survived his encounter with one of the most wanted men in the country. Seven miles up the road his patrol car sat with its red lights spinning.

Billy Cook later was asked by reporters why he did not kill the Deputy. Billy replied, *"The Deputy's wife, Cecelia, whom I had worked with for a while in Blythe had been nice to me, treated me like a human being and had been nicer to me than anyone had ever been in my life."*

A mile up the road, Cook then kidnapped another motorist, Robert H. Dewey, age 32, an oil salesman from Seattle, Washington. Robert was a war veteran and awarded the Purple Heart, serving as a Captain the Army Reserve. He left on a hunting trip. Dewey tried to wrestle the gun from Billy but he was wounded. The car left the road and moved rapidly into the desert. Billy Cook murdered Robert Dewey with a shot to the head before dumping his body in a ditch. Cook took his blue 1947 Buick Torpedo sedan with the 1950 Washington license plate A-122471. Billy had a choice of four roads open to him west of Yuma and he had a half hour head start from the Police.

By now, the FBI and all local law enforcement agencies throughout the Southwest states began a massive manhunt for Cook. From the air, the terrain lay desolate and rugged to an extreme. Every square inch of this country had to be searched. In a landscape such as this it wouldn't be too difficult for a criminally wise killer like Cook to hide.

Billy Cook headed for Mexico but returned to Blythe one last time. He kidnapped two more men, James Burke and Forrest Damron, who were amateur prospectors heading for The Chocolate Mountains to go hunting. They had left on Friday and were to return home on Sunday. Cook forced them to drive 450 miles across the Mexican Border and down to Santa Rosalia. Billy was planning to escape there to freedom. The two men's families offered an award of $500.00 for their return and the arrest of Cook when they did not return. According to Mrs. Burke, *"They were driving my husband's new maroon 1950 Studebaker sedan with California license 86A2351."* The reward money was posted with The American Consulate in Mexicali.

Helicopter patrol and jeep parties led by FBI Agents covered the roads but there were no signs of Cook, Burke or Damron. Sand dunes and drainage canals crisscrossed this vast area.

In Imperial County, District Attorney Don Bitler charged Billy Cook with the murder of Robert Dewey. In Oklahoma, Deputy Warren Smith filed five separate charges against Cook—one for each member of the Mosser family even though no bodies had been discovered yet. Smith believed that charges would stand. At the same time, the FBI in Oklahoma City charged Cook with kidnapping under the seldom used Lindbergh Law for kidnapping.

The main body of the Lindbergh Law reads:

"Whoever knowingly transports in interstate or foreign commerce any person unlawfully seized, confined, inveigled, decoyed, kidnapped, abducted carried away and held for ransom or reward or otherwise, except minors by parents, shall be pun-

*ished by death if the kidnapped person has not been liberated
unharmed and if the verdict of the jury shall be so recommend
or by imprisonment for any term of years or life."*

In October, 1950, the government had changed its mode of execution for death penalties to conform with that of the state in which the crime was committed, so if Cook would be convicted of the kidnapping of the Mosser family in Oklahoma, he would be electrocuted. The arm robbery charge against him in the hijacking of Archer in Oklahoma County also carried the maximum penalty of death in the electric chair.

Press association reports were that Cook was being hunted under orders to *"shoot to kill"* but Agent Richardson stated these were not his orders. They wanted Billy Cook brought in alive so he could be questioned as to the whereabouts of the Mosser Family bodies.

As the FBI threw all of their manpower into the hunt for Cook, more than a dozen agents had been assigned to the Imperial Valley, and at least fifty more combing the wildness south of the border. This was the largest Federal criminal operation to date.

The blockades remained north of Cook. On one side was the broad Pacific and on the other side the Gulf of California both under naval patrol. All fishing boats and ferries were closely watched.

On January 15, 1951, Police Chief Francisco Morales recognized Billy Cook in a small café, in the town of Santa Rosalia, located on the Mexican Peninsula. Morales was accompanied by Chief of Police Parra Rodriquez and walked quickly to a booth.

Rodriquez placed the muzzle of his .45 service pistol against the nape of Cook's neck and told him to stand up; with his left hand he grabbed Billy's .38 caliber revolver from Billy's belt and handed it to Chief Morales. He then took a .32 pistol from Cook's jacket pocket. Rodriquez ordered all three men against the wall and searched them. Then Chief Morales hand cuffed Cook.

It was 12:02 p.m. Pacific time and the man hunt was now ended.

Forrest Damron and James Burke identified themselves. At headquarters, Damron told how they had seen Cook standing beside his car north of San Felipe on Sunday, January 7. *"He seemed to be in trouble so we stopped to give him a lift but it wasn't until we heard a wanted bulletin on the radio that he drew his gun. He told us there had been eight passengers in three other cars he had ridden in and that all of them were dead. We weren't about to do anything foolish."*

A reward of $1,700.00 had been offered for the return of the Mosser family. Carl Mosser's wallet had been discovered just 300 hundred yards south of the road where his car had been abandoned. This was found by W. L. Lawson and his son.

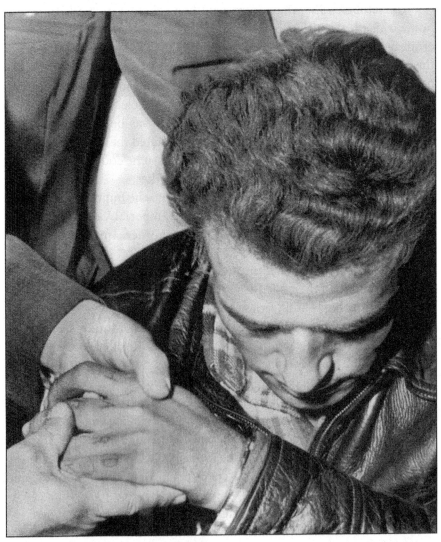

HARD LUCK: In Tijuana, Baja California,--yesterday—William E. Cook, suspected of killing eight persons, bowed his head in the Tijuana Police station as officers held up his left hand to show "Hard Luck" tattooed across his knuckles. Cook, arrested by a Mexican Officer earlier in the day, later was turned over to American authorities as an undesirable alien and was taken to jail in San Diego. Cook, subject of a chase through Southwestern United States and Mexico is accused, among other crimes, of the murder of Robert E. Dewey of Seattle. - AP Wire photo.

That same day in Joplin, Police Chief Carl Nutt and Detective Walter Gamble played a hunch. Laboratory tests on the Mosser car showed a heavy shale content. Shale and zinc mining went together. Billy Cook had been raised around Second and Olive Streets, where there were abandoned zinc mines. In one of the mines floated the bodies of the Mosser Family. Ronald Dean Mosser's prize possession was discovered—his wallet stamped "Hopalong Cassidy" and inside was a dollar bill, six dimes, and fifteen pennies, the only money Billy Cook had not taken from his victims.

Cook's father, William Cook, Sr., had made a radio appeal earlier to his son to surrender himself. He appeared at the mines when they authorities were removing the bodies. He lived less than two miles from the mines in a shack.

Los Angeles, January 19, 1951 –Manacled Bad Man reaches Los Angeles William E. Cook (center) manacled to two law enforcement officers, arrives here today from San Diego en route to Oklahoma City for trial under the Federal Lindbergh Law. He is in custody of U.S. Guard Samuel Toepfer (left) and Lt. Leland McPhie of the San Diego County Sheriff's Office. In background is George Rossini, Chief Criminal Deputy of the U. S. Marshall's Office here. (AP Wirephoto)

"God help Bill for doing anything like this. It's sure awful, ain't it?"

Billy Cook was returned to the border and handed over to FBI Agents. Despite the killing of the Mosser family, the Federal authorities and The United States Justice Department turned Billy Cook over to the California Courts, which tried Billy only for the murder of Robert Dewey.

Back in the United States, Cook was ruled unfit to stand trial by four psychiatrists, although three found him sane enough to participate in his own legal proceedings. Billy showed no remorse in this killing or the others. A Federal judge presiding over Cook's case determined while Billy was sane enough to enter a guilty plea—he was not sane enough to receive the death penalty. Billy Cook was found guilty after 50 minutes, by eight women and four men, for the brutal killings of the Mosser family. He half smirked as he was sentenced to a total of 300 years in Alcatraz. Upon hearing the verdict, the prosecutor stormed the courtroom claiming it

El Centro, Calif., Nov. 20, 1951—Cook talks to Defense Attorney John Connolly (right) of Oklahoma City as he is led to the courtroom for his sanity trial in connection with the slaying of Robert H. Dewey, Seattle Salesman. At the left, manacled to Cook, is 6 foot 4 inch Deputy Sheriff Wesley L. Minar. (AP Wire photo)

was, *"the God damnedest travesty of justice, ever!"* The Justice Department agreed and handed cook over to California authorities to be tried for the murder of Robert Dewey.

Attorney John Connolly made his last appeal for Cook's life. He told the court that his death sentence should be changed to life in prison because Billy was obviously insane. He sat brooding in his cell. Billy refused to talk to anyone, still disobedient to the very end.

Cook received the death penalty for the killing of Robert Dewey. During the last day of his life Billy Cook was only interested in what was on the menu for his last meal. Appeals had been exhausted and he was executed in the gas chamber on December 12, 1951 at 10:06 a.m. at San Quentin Prison. A grim Billy was strapped to the chair and eagerly inhaled the cyanide fumes. He was 23 years old and his short and crazed life was now over.

Billy Cook's murders were not the typical act of a serial killer, having been committed over a couple of weeks with a gun. Billy was classified as a spree killer, a category of impulsive and emotionally tormented individuals who go on murderous road trips. Cook was tried, convicted and sentenced to death within one year.

No one wanted to claim his body. Glen Boydstun was given permission by William Cook, Sr., to finally claim Billy's body. Boydstun displayed the body at his funeral home and charged admission. It was reported that 5,000 people including children passed by the casket for one last look at the hitch-hiker killer.

Billy's body was later returned to other Cook Family members in Joplin. His family felt that Boydstun was capitalizing on his death. Billy was finally laid to rest during brief night time rites given by Rev. Dow Booe. Illuminated by flashlights and lanterns, Billy was buried in a secluded spot in graveyard with other family members at the Peace Church Cemetery near Joplin Missouri. His grave was soon vandalized and the tomb stone stolen.

His body was exhumed and reburied in an undisclosed location on the cemetery property. Over the years, there have been reports, at this abandoned and rundown cemetery, of strange sounds and voices that have been heard in the cemetery.

There have also been reports of eerie lights and that a ghostly figure with red eyes has been seen lurking in the trees, peering out at passersby and then vanishing into an unmarked grave. It has been further reported by *The Joplin Globe* that paranormal groups have investigated this ceme-

tery over the years and they have measured strange magnetic fluctuations in the cemetery.

And, those who live in the area know who this is buried in this unmarked grave. This restless spirit emerges and it is said to be William E. Cook.

Lupino Noir and The Filmakers

IDA LUPINO'S FIRST PRODUCTION COMPANY was named Emerald Productions after her mother, Constance O'Shea. Connie's stage name was Emerald. Ida had been married from 1938 to 1945 to actor Louis Hayward. After her divorce from Hayward, Ida met and fell in love with Collier Young. He was working at the time for Columbia Pictures as a executive assistant under Harry Cohen.

Ida and Collier were married in 1948. Lupino, Young and Anson Bond of Bond's Clothing formed Emerald Productions, in 1950.

"I had largely given up on acting and turned to producing and directing. This gave me the freedom to call my own shots. My objective was to turn out independent productions that were high in quality but low cost films with provocative subject matter—films that delivered a message by doing so and not being so preachy. I wanted to make films with good stories and new faces. Believe me, I fought to produce my own pictures. I really just thought that a woman directing was an oddity but I never felt I was on a crusade for a cause!" Ida Lupino stated.

Bond later decided that film production was too risky of a business. He sold his share of the partnership to screen writer Malvin Wald. The company name was then changed to The Filmakers, a defining statement of intent.

The Emerald/Filmakers productions met with mixed success at the box office, although the little critical attention they did receive was on the whole favorable.

Filmakers Ad featuring Wald, Lupino and Young – Credit: The Filmakers

The Filmakers company lasted as a production entity from 1949 to 1954. During this period of time, the company made eight feature films. Collier Young served as the company's President, Ida was the Vice President, and Malvin Wald functioned as the Business Manager. Wald also wrote the original screenplay for *Not Wanted* and the original screenplay for *Outrage*.

Filmakers was an independent film company specializing in documentary-style films. "*We chose controversial socially conscious issues for themes of our movies—rape, bigamy, polio and unwed motherhood. We produced eight films*," added Ida.

Not Wanted (1949) is the story of an unwed woman. "*I co-authored the script with Paul Jarrico. I had to use my star power and negotiate with the Production Code representatives to get Not Wanted made. The Production Code Administration was in full force. I held a press conference which generated industry publicity. I stated, 'Movie censors aren't big ugly beasts after all but nice broadminded human beings.'*"

Several other films followed. *Never Fear* (1949), about a young woman suffering with polio and *Outrage* (1950), with its subject of rape. *Hard Fast and Beautiful* (1951) explored the underworld of champion tennis. *The Bigamist* (1953) was the story of a man married to two totally different women. *Beware My Lovely* (1952) was the story of a lone woman held captive in her home at Christmas by a mad man. *Private Hell 36* (1954) written by Ida and Collier Young was geared towards greed and cops. This was Filmakers' last film.

Filmakers came to an end after it took on the distribution of its own productions.

"*We were doing fine but we made one final mistake. We were talked into the distribution business. I opposed them every step of the way. We are creative people, we were picture-making people, I argued. We knew nothing about distribution. Let's stay away from it. I was out voted and pretty soon we were out of business.*"

"*Those were thrilling days for us. We co-wrote and co-produced and I went on to direct each succeeding film. We discovered new talent. We took topics that were pretty daring for the times. We would shoot these films in about thirteen days,*" Ida stated.

Ida was considered a director with a strong female identity. These were sensational subjects for the time, but they were treated with restraint and with unsentimental realism—a true break from Hollywood aesthetics.

Ida Lupino and Collier Young

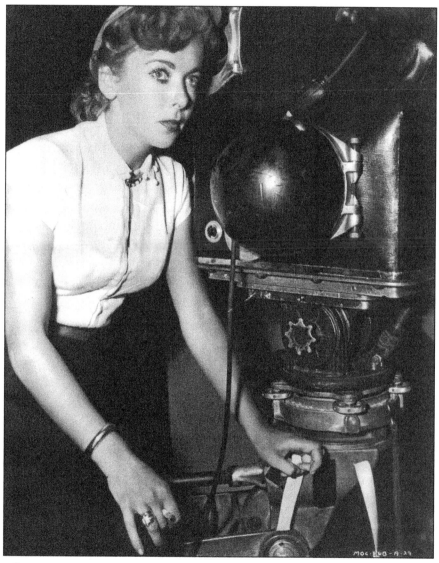

"I never saw myself as any advance guard or feminist. I enjoyed discovering new talent and bringing it to the screen. I worked at my best when I had creative freedom!" – Ida Lupino (Photo Credit: RKO Radio Pictures – Filmakers)

"As a screenwriter and director, Ida Lupino had an eye for the emotional truth within the taboo or mundane, making a series of 'B' styled pictures which featured sympathetic, honest portrayals of such controversial subjects as unmarried mothers, bigamy and rape."

– John Krewson, Critic

Ida Lupino and Collier Young could produce pictures of greater importance and impact by bringing power and excitement to the screen. The Hitch-Hiker shows that Ida could handle a rough all-male thriller just as skillfully as one of her mentors and close friend, Rauol Walsh. She also was an admirer of Allan Dwan, Fritz Lang and Cinematographer George Barnes.

Ida was known as an extremely talented maverick but regarded in the industry as being difficult. Collier Young spoke about Ida, "*Things aren't normal unless Ida resigns three times on every picture—once before the picture starts and twice during production. She always was calm on the set but at home if I told her she was going over budget she would throw a bottle at me!*"

Prime example of Noir. (The Louis Antonelli Collection)

"This is a prime example of the subtle use of degrees of over-exposure in the daytime, desert scenes. Notice the 'hot spots' of elements in the shot, such as the foreground cliff, Meyer's leather jacket, the gun barrels, and brows of the performers.

This is very sophisticated and builds in intensity by degrees—reaching its peak of the gun. O'Brien's mental and spiritual collapses when he sees and hears the high flying plane overhead, and pleads with God for his screaming to be heard. In this film there is only one cynical reply for his plea and tears Meyer's, "Leave him alone, can't you see he's—pray'in." Brutal, even for the bleak black, midnight of Noir."

– Louis Antonelli

The Film Noir Encyclopedia's entry on *The Hitch-Hiker* credits the writing of *The Hitch-Hiker* so Noir:

"As with Vanning in Nightfall, the upheaval of the lives of Collins and Bowen is sudden, ill-chanced and impersonal – a typical Noir reflection of the lack of security and stability in everyday living, no matter how common place."

The Hitch-Hiker is considered to be the first Film Noir directed by a woman, despite the fact that Norwegian director, Edith Carlmar, had made a noir in 1949 titled: *Dogen er et kjaertegan.*

Ida was able to reduce the male to the same sort of dangerous, irrational force that women represented in the most male directed examples of Hollywood Film Noir. Later these films were dubbed *"Lupino Noir."*

Ida Lupino paved the way for well known woman directors such as Kathryn Bigelow, Barbra Streisand, Diane Keaton, Jodi Foster and even Kathy Bates.

Ida on the set on location

The Making of
The Hitch-Hiker Film

FROM THE IDA LUPINO FBI FILE:

Released under the Freedom of Information Act
FBI FILE: **September 18, 1952** *Teletype*

RKOS STUDIOS DASH RESEARCH MATTERS. ATTEN-
TION ASSISTANT DIRECTOR NICHOLS, WILLIAM
FEEDER, DIRECTOR PUBLIC RELATIONS, IDA LUPINO
ACTRESS AND PRODUCER LEWIS RACHMILL, DI-
RECTOR, ALL RKO, ADVISED NINE SEVENTEEN LAST
THAT RKO HAS IN PRODUCTION A FICTIONAL FILM
ENTITLED 'THE DIFFERENCE' PRODUCED BY LUPI-
NO, THAT THIS FILM WAS CONSIDERED AS A DOCU-
MENTARY ENTITLED "THE COOK STORY" BASED ON
THE CASE OF WILLIAM EDWARD COOK, JR. REBU-
FILE EIGHTYEIGHT DASH FIVE EIGHT SIX NINE, LA
FILE EIGHTY EIGHT DASH ONE TWO SEVEN NINE,
THAT CURRENT PRODUCTION SOMEWHAT PARAL-
LELS ACTIVITIES OF COOK BUT DOES NOT IDENTIFY
AS SUCH. ABOVE DESIRED TO KNOW IF FBI AGENTS
HAD JURISDICTION IN COOK CASE, ALSO DESIRED
TO KNOW WHAT PROCEDURE FBI AGENTS USED
IN QUESTIONING CERTAIN INDIVIDUALS DURING
INVESTIGATION OF SIMILAR CASES, WHETHER OR

NOT AGENTS COOPERATED CLOSELY WITH LOCAL POLICE CASES THIS TYPE SO THAT THE FILM COULD BE AUTHENTIC AND NO OFFENSE CREATED IN INCORRECT PORTRAYAL OF FBI AGENTS. QUESTIONS ASKED WHETHER FBI WOULD

END PAGE ONE INDEXED - 153

53 OCT 3-1952

TELETYPE

PAGE TWO

EXAMINE SCRIPTS AND OFFER SUGGESTIONS. ALL ABOVE WERE ADVISED OF BUREAU POLICY THAT ANY REQUESTS THIS SORT SHOULD BE REFERRED TO BUREAU DIRECT. NO COMMITMENTS MADE THIS OFFICE AND ONLY INFORMATION FURNISHED WAS GENERAL INFORMATION RELATING TO FBI JURISDICTION IN KIDNAPPING AND UFAP CASES. MR. FEEDER ADVISED THAT BUREAU HAD BEEN CONTACTED IN APRIL, FIFTY TWO BY MR. J.B. BRECHEEN, BRANCH MANAGER, RKO, DISTRIBUTING AGENCY. WASHINGTON D.C. RE USE OF CERTAIN NAMES TO BE GIVEN AGENTS IN PICTURE. FEEDER ALSO ADVISED THAT IT WAS POSSIBLE THAT ACTORS USED IN FILM MIGHT NOT BE INDENTIFIED SPECIFICALLY AS FBI AGENTS BUT ONLY AS FEDERAL AGENTS. THAT IF ACTORS WERE PORTRAYED AS FBI AGENTS THAT IT WOULD BE POSSIBLE THAT HE WOULD HAVE RKO REPRESENTATIVE CONTACT BUREAU PERSONALLY IN WASHINGTON OR THAT HE HIMSELF MIGHT PHONE ASSISTANT NICHOLS DIRECT. FEEDER STATES THAT SHOOTING ON THIS PICTURE SCHEDULED WITHIN TEN DAYS FOR INFORMATION.
Carson
END

LA R 9 WA DBD
ALSO REPLAY

Geoffrey Sherlock from the Motion Picture Association telephoned Ida's office, Filmakers, with strong objections opposing the making of *The Hitch-Hiker* film. The Production Code prohibited screen depiction of contemporary notorious criminals. Filmakers went forward anyway, informing the papers that film rights had been obtained not only from the kidnapped victims, but from William "Billy" Cook, Jr. himself.

The Motion Picture Association of America was started in 1922 as a trade organization for the American film industry. Their task was to curb criticism of American films of the era and give a favorable image of the film industry.

In 1945, following World War II, its counterpart, the Motion Picture Export Association of America, was formed to restore the American film market and fight trade barriers and restrictions imposed on American films.

The Motion Picture Production Code was the set of industry moral censorship guidelines that governed the production of most United States motion pictures released by studios starting in 1930. It was also known as the Hays Code, after Hollywood's chief censor, Will H. Hays.

The Production Code spelled out what was acceptable content for a public audience in the United States. *The Hitch-Hiker*, based on the murders of William E. Cook was not acceptable.

More trouble for Ida. In March, James V. Bennett, an official with the Bureau of Prisons, sent an angry letter to Joseph Breen about the *"under handed trick"* of obtaining William Cook's release for this picture. He urged the Motion Picture Association to withhold approval. Ida and Collier defended their actions. In a letter to Bennett they stated that they paid Cook' s attorney three thousand dollars for a *"valid and legal release."* In addition, there would be no bloodshed in the film.

"To appease The Hays Office I reduced the number of deaths from six to three," stated Ida.

The Federal Bureau of Prisons is a Federal law enforcement agency subdivision of the United States Department of Justice and is responsible for the administration of the Federal prison system.

The system also handles prisoners who committed acts considered felonies under the District of Columbia's law. The bureau was established in 1930 to provide more progressive and humane care for federal inmates, to professionalize the prison services and to ensure consistent and centralized administration of the eleven Federal prisons in operation at the time.

Ida Lupino went to see Billy Cook before he was executed.

"I wanted to see Billy and tell him I was making a film about him. With special permission from my buddies at the FBI, I entered San Quentin under strict security. I was allowed to see Billy Cook briefly for safety issues. I found San Quentin to be cold, dark and a very scary place inside. In fact, I was told by Collie (Collier Young) not to go; it was not safe."

"I needed a release from Billy Cook to do our film about him. My company, Filmakers, paid $3,000.00 to his attorney for exclusive rights to his story. I found Billy to be cold and aloof. I was afraid of him. Billy Cook had 'Hard Luck' tattooed on the fingers of his left hand and a deformed right eyelid that would never close completely. I could not wait to get the hell out of San Quentin!"

The Federal Bureau of Prisons and the Motion Picture Association still would not allow a film based on the murders of William Cook; *"No picture shall be dealing with the life of a notorious criminal of current or past time which uses the name, nick name or alias of such."*

Filmakers had no choice but to fictionalize the story and delete all references to William Cook greatly changing the story and making the plot predictable. Daniel Mainwaring apparently contributed to the screenplay but due to House Un-American Activities Committee investigations, RKO refused to give Mainwaring any screen credit.

HUAC was an investigative committee of the United States House of Representatives. It was created in 1938 to investigate alleged disloyalty and subversive activities on the part of private citizens, public employees and those organizations suspected of having communist ties.

Ida Lupino, *"I co-wrote the screenplay, titled 'The Difference' with Collier during the last months of our marriage. The working script was titled 'The Persuader.' Later, Collier and I changed the title to 'The Hitch-Hiker' for better box office appeal."*

The Hitch-Hiker was filmed, mainly on location by Ida Lupino and Filmakers, after her divorce from Collier Young. Lupino and Young would remain business partners in Filmakers and friends even after their divorce in October 1951. Ida's quick marriage to Howard Duff was in the same month.

This film represents a return to the director's chair for Ida after a two-year hiatus.

"I hadn't directed a film in a very long time and I was concerned about directing this picture with an all male cast but Collier persuaded me to direct this picture."

"The filming of The Hitch-Hiker went smoothly in spite of my relent-

less pacing during the filming for I had divorced Collier Young and I was recently married to Duff with a new baby at home," Ida added.

It was reported all went well on the set but there was an atmosphere of real violence in the film, not only the subject matter but in the use of Lupino's hyperkinetic camera set ups and omniscient camera angles, along with her intense close-ups and low key action which formed a taught drama.

Ida Lupino stated, *"To heighten the films suspense, I shot scenes in the claustrophobic confides of the car and to intensify the grit outside on hot, lost barren expanses of the desert."*

Cameraman Nicholas Musuraca filmed black and white imagery that enhances the moody aridness of the brutal desert heat with his use of key lighting, suggested to him by Ida Lupino; deep shadows heighten the tension. The 1940s style of unparalleled cinematography by Musuraca stands out.

"I tried to keep the film viewer on the edge of their seat with the threat of violence about to explode at any moment," commented Ida.

This is a tense thriller skillfully directed by Ida with her documentary approach which created a suspenseful tale of horror on the highways. Who else but Ida Lupino could make a car appear so dominating and intimidating as it travels the isolated dirt roads through the back lands of Mexico?

"I had to do something dramatic to achieve this effect of suspense so I chose a documentary style of direction." I also had the Mexican actors speak in Spanish," commented Ida.

Ida accomplished much with such a low budget, under $200,000, both in front and behind the camera—like all of her films.

The Hitch-Hiker went into production on June 24, 1952 and finished production in late July of the same year. Location shooting took place in the Alhambra Hills near Lone Pine and Big Pine, California. Lone Pine is a very legendary area for film production. The film *High Sierra* was shot there.

"Lone Pine was a very hot location setting, the extreme heat was hard on the cast and crew. I had a few pills (unpleasant and boring persons) on the set but for the most part we got along," said Ida.

Trash cans of soda pop on ice, along with Ida's bulky, industry standard 35 mm Mitchell camera, are evidence that *The Hitch-Hiker* was shot under extremely complex circumstances.

Ida liked to dress in a sleeveless blouse, dungarees, sneakers and a checkered baseball hat topped her head with her hair tied back.

"My total working wardrobe while directing this picture consisted of three pairs of blue jeans, some assorted blouses, a cap, a pair of tennis shoes and some socks."

Ida recalled and added, *"Not only is directing a fascinating occupation but sartorially speaking, it's simpler and less expensive than being a star!"*

"My hand bag fell to the ground and spilled one day while on location. *"Edmond O'Brien gallantly knelt to the ground, retrieved the following items and while doing so he made an inventory of the following that was in my purse: 1 tooth brush, a bottle of vitamins, 1 powder puff, 1 compact, 1 mascara, 1 package of Kleenex, 1 pencil sharpener, 1 bottle salt tablets, six pencils, 1 red crayon, 1 comb, 2 pairs of sun glasses, 2 pairs of socks, 4 pages of typed written dialogue, 1 package of chewing gum, 2 family photos, 1 rabbits foot, 1 scratch pad, and 1 bottle of sun lotion."*

With a bow, O'Brien returned Ida's property and smilingly remarked; *"You may be a motion picture director who knows exactly what you want but fundamentally you're just another dame. Typical of your sex, you carry all sorts of junk in your pocket book."*

Ida stated she closed her purse and replied, *"You're just a cynic about women—back to work, O'Brien!"*

Edmond O'Brien never felt strange at all about being directed by Ida Lupino, Hollywood's foremost director at the time. The husky star revealed that a woman director was nothing new in his career. Edmond O' Brien appeared on the Broadway stage under the direction of Margaret Webster.

The Toledo Blade
TAKING ORDERS FROM A GAL IS OK IF SHE'S
IDA LUPINO
Hollywood May 16, 1958 (UP)

Three stalwart Hollywood Actors, Edmond O'Brien, Frank Lovejoy and William Talman, believe that taking orders from most women can be a bit deflating to the male ego. But not so, they agree, when that woman is the fast-talking, chain-smoking Ida Lupino.

"I never gave it a thought when they told me the director in the picture was to be a female," said O'Brien. "I only knew I had intense admiration for the Lupino name in the business and that was good enough for me. If a director was good that's all I ask, and I had no doubt in the world that Miss Lupino knew her job."

Talman, who plays the gun-happy killer in the picture, said he was mostly impressed by his shapely director's ability

On the set of *The Hitch-Hiker* Ida Lupino, 1952 (The Louis Antonelli Collection)

to thrive on the rugged existence in the mountainous country-side where the film was shot.

"Despite the changeable weather and physical hardships, there was never an apprehensive sound out of her," he said. "She was one of the gang; in fact our leader, who met everything with an unbeatable—sense of humor. She set the pace for the seventy men who made up the troupe, and held it."

The three leading men, Talman, O'Brien and Lovejoy stated they were amused when they received a call from Collier Young, the producer of *The Hitch-Hiker*, asking if they had any reservations about accepting a woman's direction?

"It was Ida who was uneasy about the whole woman versus man thing, not us."

Lovejoy said, *"We told Collier Young to tell her to relax."*

In his appraisal of Ida Lupino, Lovejoy struck a human note when he said; *"She's the prettiest Director I've ever worked for. And, I'd like to say that it was a pleasure to be able to call my director 'honey' and 'doll,'"* added Lovejoy. *"I was never able to do that with Mike Curtiz. Somehow, he didn't seem the type!"*

The Makers

Producer: Collier Young
Director: Ida Lupino
Associate Producer: Christian Nyby
Music: Leith Stevens
Screenplay: Ida Lupino and Collier Young
Screen Adaptation: Robert Joseph
Written by Daniel Mainwaring (unaccredited)
Director of Photography: Nicholas Musuraca, A.S.C.
Photographic Effects: Harold E. Wellman, A.S.C.
Art Directors: Albert S. D'Agostino and Walter E. Keller
Musical Director: C. Bakaleinikoff
Film Editor: Douglas Stewart
Set Decorations: Darrell Sivera and Harley Miller
Sound by Roy Meadows and Clem Portman
Makeup Artist: Mel Berns
Assistants to Producer: James Anderson and Robert Eggenweiler
Assistant Director: William Dorfman
Production: The Filmakers, Inc. – RKO Radio Pictures, Inc.
Distribution: RKO Radio Pictures, Inc.
Sound: Mono (RCA Sound System)
Premiere date: March 21, 1953
Release date: April 29, 1953
Running time: 71 minutes

THE ORIGINAL SCREENPLAY, titled *The Persuader,* written by Robert Joseph is about two old army buddies who are on a fishing trip and pick up a mysterious male hitch-hiker during a trip to Mexico.

The plot was based on the story *Out of the Past,* written by screenwriter Daniel Mainwaring. He was blacklisted at the time and did not receive screen credit. This was written during the McCarthy's witch-hunt. Howard R. Hughes, who released *The Hitch-Hiker* under his studio RKO refused to give credit to any "radicals."

Ida took Daniel Mainwaring's work and did a complete re-write, changing the title to *The Difference* and then to *The Hitch-Hiker.* Ida and

1953 Belgium litho

Collier based their screenplay on the true life story of William Edward Cook, Jr., the 23 year old psychopathic spree killer.

The Hitch-Hiker starred Edmond O'Brien, Frank Lovejoy and William Talman.

Cameo appearances in *The Hitch-Hiker* include Clark Howatt as the Government Agent and Collier Young himself, appearing as a Mexican peasant.

"*When directing Edmond O'Brien, Frank Lovejoy and William Talman for a scene for The Hitch-Hiker, I noticed a Mexican peon 'extra' in the background that I had never seen before. I demanded to know who the 'extra' was since the script did not call for his presence.*

As he raised his big sombrero it was Collier Young, our producer of the picture.

'I thought I would act in the picture just for luck,' Collier told his pretty director, co-writer and now his ex-wife.

I permitted him to stay in the scene but it was no Academy Award winning performance," Ida told Collier later.

THE CAST:

Edmond O'Brien as Roy Collins
Frank Lovejoy as Gilbert Bowen
William Talman as Emmett Myers
Jose Torvay as Captain Alvardo
Wendell Niles as Himself
Jean Del Val as Inspector General
Clark Howart as Government Agent
Natividad Vacio as Jose
Rodney Bell as William Johnson
Nacho Galindo as Proprietor
Collier Young as Mexican Peasant

EDMOND O'BRIEN

Edmond O'Brien was of Irish and English ancestry and born in New York, growing up in the Bronx. He served in the U. S. Army Air Forces. Edmond learned the craft of performance as a magician reportedly tutored by his neighbor, the great Harry Houdini.

Edmond O'Brien in the hitch-hiker's leather jacket.
(RKO Radio Pictures – Filmakers)

Edmond began performing magic tricks in high school but later decided to try acting. After graduation he went on to study drama at Columbia University.

He was best remembered for his role in *D.O.A.* (1950)

Edmond was a favorite of Ida's in her B movie auteur period and worked together with him later on television in *Four Star Playhouse*.

"It's very satisfying to portray many types of roles, often your own identity gets lost. Seldom does a producer say, 'This is an Eddie O'Brien part, except for Ida Lupino."

As Collins in *The Hitch-Hiker* to Emmett Meyer, *"I guess we won't be having rabbit for dinner!"* *"Meyers, You're nothing without that gun without it you are finished!"*

In 1954, O'Brien won an Academy Award for Best supporting Actor in *The Barefoot Contessa*.

> "Ida, what a doll—we starred together in *The Bigamist* and later worked together an episode of Four Star Playhouse.
>
> "While the rewards may be great in fame and financially for stars, the work becomes monotonous. No actor who portrays himself is a happy person."
>
> – Edmond O'Brien

O'Brien died of Alzheimer's Disease on May 9, 1985 in Inglewood, California.

FRANK LOVEJOY

An American actor in radio, film and television, Lovejoy was raised in the Bronx and grew up in New Jersey. As a successful radio actor, Lovejoy was heard on the 1930 crime drama series *Gang Busters*.

Frank was a narrator during the first season for the show, *This Is Your FBI*.

He starred later in the newspaper drama series *Night Beat* in the early 1950s and appeared in episodes of *Suspense* before portraying Gilbert Bowen in *The Hitch-Hiker*.

Frank Lovejoy was a strong believer in two careers in one family. His wife was Joan Banks, who frequently appeared with him on radio and had a screen career for herself. The Lovejoys met while rehearsing in the same play. They celebrated twelve years of married life while he was making *The Hitch-Hiker*.

Lovejoy gives this film heart; you sympathize with his character, Bowen, when he attempts to protect and reassure the little Mexican girl when the three travelers stop at a market to stock up on supplies. *"Go, you are with God little one!"*

> "This took place early in the picture, within the early stages of the script and was (to be) the protagonist's stop along their way to the night club they had known before the war. The set

Cut Scene

up for this scene was given for the audience by dialog between the two men in the car...as they speak of a woman 'Flora-Belle' who was somehow associated with the night club. From the car, this scene was to transition to the interior of the club."

"Ida Lupino had misgivings about it but the other actors seemed to be ok with it. It was blocked and photographed very quickly, with the overall friendliness for O'Brien's character... through a counterpart of tension and discomfort from Lovejoy's character."

"Late during the production, Ida did say several times that she did not think the night club scene would make it into the picture. This scene would of slowed the established pacing, and used key minutes delaying the arrival of Meyer's [The Hitch-Hiker] for the audience, which they were naturally anticipating. Ida made the correct decision not to use this scene... as any wise director would do."

– Louis Antonelli

WILLIAM TALMAN

Talman's self-effacing, though controlling, performance as Emmet Myers is best realized in the camp scene when he demands to see Gil Bowan's watch. He's leaning against a tree as Bowen and Collins get a fire going.

As he examines the watch, Talman states, "*I had a watch when I was 17. Nobody gave it to me. I just took it, knocked off a broken down jewelry store in jerk town outside of Tulsa. It was a cinch.*"

Meyers draws closer. "*You guys are soft. Know what makes you that way? You're up to your necks in I.O.U.s. You're suckers. You're scared to get out on your own—you've always had it good, so you're soft. Well not me.*

"*Better go fishing while you have the chance… You guys are really fools!*"
(RKO Radio Pictures – The Filmakers)

They never gave me anything, so I don't owe anybody. My folks were tough. When I was born, they took one look at this pus eye, they told me to get lost. I didn't need them—any of them. I did it my way!"

"*Emmet Myer's right eye is permanently open, never allowing them to know if he is really asleep or just faking – something he does regularly to scare them. He lets Bowen and Collins take off and then he meets up with them, in the car, just as they have escaped from him,*" Talman adds.

For this role Talman had to assume the appearance of having a paralyzed right eye.

"*This was a painful process. Each morning a rubber piece was placed over my right eyelid with liquid adhesive. This just about drove me crazy but I felt the part was well worth it.!*"

This result gave him the look of the eye never shutting.

William Talman thought his role of the maniacal hitch-hiker in *The Hitch-Hiker* was just about the biggest break he could have received at his stage of his screen work. He had worked at a variety of jobs before deciding upon an acting career. In his native Detroit, he was a clerk, an automobile salesman, a laborer in an iron foundry and shipyard, and a tennis instructor. Talman asked Ida if by any chance he could live at the end of the taut suspense drama.

"*In all five pictures I've done in Hollywood, I've played death scenes. It's not that I mind dying in films but it offends my mother, who is my chief fan. For her sake I'd like to be living at least once in the final fadeout.*"

For the moment, Ida had good news for Talman's mother when she told him he'd be alive at the thrilling finale of *The Hitch-Hiker*, but on your way to prison and the death house, Ida added.

Cast as the murderous kidnapper Emmet Myers, Taman "*makes the most of one of the years juiciest assignments,*" wrote *The \New York Times*: "*He is a braggart who taunts his captives, mocks their softness and proclaims that 'you can get anything at the end of the gun.'*"

Talman's powerful performance has film fans looking forward to Rutger Hauer's portrayal in Robert Harmon's 1984 *The Hitcher* and Dennis Hopper in just about everything he's starred in since *Blue Velvet*.

In an interview, Talman recalled an incident that happened shortly after the release of *The Hitch-Hiker*, in which he gave a chilling portrayal of the escaped murderer and serial killer, Emmett Meyers.

As Talman was driving his convertible down a street in Los Angeles with the top down, he stopped at a red light. Another driver in a convertible stopped next to him and stared at him for a few seconds, then said,

"*You're the hitch-hiker, right?*" Talman then nodded, indicating that he was. The other driver got out of his car, went over to Talman's car and slapped him across the face, then got back in his car and drove off.

In recalling this story, Talman said, "*You know, I never won an Academy Award but I guess that was as close as I will ever come to one.*"

Talman later went on to portray Hamilton Berger, the opposing council in the television series classic written by Earl Stanley Garner, *Perry Mason*. His character only won one case against the famed attorney, on a technicality. Barbara Hale (Della Street in the Perry Mason television series) commented, "*I was always grateful to Ida for giving Bill his big break!*"

Ida recalled, "*When I was casting Bill Talman I went against type— Billy Cook was short and of a stocky build. He had a cleft pallet and his one eye that never did close. Bill Talman was tall, lean and older.*"

Film Publicity

RKO Radio Pictures distributed *The Hitch-Hiker*. This studio promoted the film by stating it contained dramatic wallop because it is REAL. The facts are actual. What is shown on the screen could of happened to YOU!

RKO PRESS AD:
He's waiting... just waiting... to thumb another down the road to death!
There he stands... waiting to add to America's list of highway atrocities!
His story screams with thrills... yet every startling scene is true!
When was the last time you gambled with death?

The story comes to the screen right out of the newspaper headlines. With terrifying conviction it depicts an amazing adventure by two Americans when they start on a carefree vacation and wind up as hostages of a hitch-hiker murderer.

Their journey is fraught with terror as they try to outwit their captor, knowing that he plans to kill them when they reach their destination. Suspense never slackens as they proceed on their weird journey through the picturesque Mexican wastelands. The climax will make any audience hold its breath

The Hitch-Hiker USA Press book

A grimly realistic and terrifying thriller, highlighted by mounting suspense and memorable portrayals by Edmond O'Brien, Frank Lovejoy and William Talman.

In numerous aspects *The Hitch-Hiker* story parallels a man-hunt which occupied the Nation's headlines in 1950s. It pulls no punches in depicting the experiences of two typical law abiding citizens when they pick up a hitch-hiker only to discover that he is a sadistic murderer. He holds the two men as hostages to aid him in escaping the law—in a mad dash across Mexico to Central America. There is both action and emotional drama in efforts to outwit him before they reach their destination and their threatened death.

How these two hostages manage to outwit the trigger-happy gunman during their nightmarish journey, knowing that death awaits them at their final destination if the hitch-hiker is not captured. This provides tense drama and continuous action.

Leith Steven's brass-heavy scoring brimming over with trumpets as a counterpart to the cars' horn and string basses portending doom with the what legendary movie composer David Raksin called "fifth boding."

Sound technicians Roy Meadows and Clem Portman mixed the films score; sound effects and dialogue superbly employing a rich bass and full robust midrange.

The Hitch-Hiker is the fifth picture directed by Ida Lupino and definitely establishes this fine actress as one of Hollywood's truly competent directors. She has done an outstanding job of building excitement and suspense to almost astonishing pitch. The fact that Ida directed this picture in outdoors in a desert setting rather than on studio sound stages with backdrops gives it completely believable quality at all times.

The Hollywood trade press has classified this picture among the best in suspense melodrama division and praised co-stars Edmond O'Brien, and Frank Lovejoy as *"Oscar candidates for their work."*

Suspense Is Key To New RKO Film
(Current Reader)
A horror-filled flight across the rugged terrain of Mexico experienced by two Americans as they are held as hostages as the point of a gun by a highway killer forms the suspenseful basis for *The Hitch-Hiker* at the theater.

'Suspenseful…wire tight…top flight!' – *Film Bulletin*

'Excellently conceived and acted…Starring trio talent…production excellent!' – *Variety*

British Trade Ad – *Kine Weekly*, June 1953

'Tops in tension! The Hitch-Hiker will rank among the best in the suspense melodrama division. From its main title cards to its final fadeout, it never lets up…William Talman is sensational…Frank Lovejoy and Edmond O'Brien are excellent…Ida Lupino deserves great credit for an outstanding job of building excitement to an almost untenable pitch!'

– *Hollywood Reporter*

Not since Richard Widmark hit the screen as the laughing killer in *Kiss of Death* has there been a screen character so fascinatingly evil as that of William Talman's portrayal of *The Hitch-Hiker*.

The Hitch-Hiker premiered in Boston, Massachusetts on March 21, 1953 and went into general release on April 29, 1953. Viewers would be talking about this picture long after its showing.

It was marketed with the tag line: *When was the last time you invited death into your car?*

In a related story line, law enforcement officials in the United States and Mexico combine forces, in a race against time, in hopes of apprehending Meyer and preventing more crimes.

This gives this film its documentary style; Ida's choice of direction for this picture.

The New York Times gave *The Hitch-Hiker* a mixed review on its initial release. The acting, direction and use of locations were praised but the plot deemed to be predictable.

The film's major flaw is an ending that does not reach a satisfying climax worthy of all that has come before. A massive manhunt by both U.S. and Mexican law enforcement, on the same scale, according to *Time* magazine, of the manhunt for John Dillinger results in Myers capture is played very low key.

Ida Lupino, Hollywood's sole female filmmaker of the 1950s, directs an all male cast in a taught, 70 minute thriller. Frank Lovejoy and Edmond O'Brien are two war buddies taking a break from the wives for a Mexican fishing trip; a hitchhiker they pick up turns out to be a crazed killer wanted in nine states. William Talman forces them at gunpoint to drive them through the desert.

–*Filmakers*

Talman's Everett Meyer's is a fascinatingly abstract creation, filmed by Ida Lupino first as a discorporate flurry of hands and feet, then as a satanic figure whose grinning, key-lighted face seems to float by itself in space. With his paralyzed right eye (he sleeps with it wide open) Myers may represent the return of the fascist evil the two men confronted during the war; he may also represent something inherently violent in the American male that having been liberated by the war, has to be faced down and defeated by the two Vets before they can return to a normal life.

> Lupino's use of the desert setting, rich with associations of nuclear devastation seems to look forward to the science fiction films that would flourish later in the decade."
> – Dave Kehr

> *The Hitch-Hiker*'s desert locale, although not so graphically dark as a cityscape at night, isolates the protagonists in a milieu as uninviting and potentially deadly as any in film noir.
> – Bob Porfiero and Alain Silver

> It's a pleasure to watch the action unfold without resorting to clichés. Talman's performance as a sadistic sleaze was powerful. His random crime spree strikes the heart of middle-class American's insecurity about there being no place free of crime.
> – Dennis Schwartz, Film Critic

> *The Hitch-Hiker*, arguably Lupino's best film and the only true Noir directed by a woman, two utterly average middle-class men are held at gunpoint and slowly psychologically broken by a serial killer. In addition to her critical but compassionate sensibility, Lupino had a great filmmakers eye, using gorgeous, ever present loneliness of empty highways in *the Hitch-Hiker* to set her characters apart.
> – John Krewson, Film Critic

> *Time Out Film Guide* wrote of *The Hitch-Hiker*,
> Absolutely assured in her creation of bleak, noir atmosphere—whether in the claustrophobic confines of a car, or

lost in the arid expanses of the desert—Lupino never relaxes the tension for one moment. Yet her emotional sensitivity is also upfront; charting changes in the menaced men's relationship as they bicker about how to deal with their captor, stressing that only through friendship can they survive. Taught, tough and entirely without macho-glorification, it's a gem with first-class performances from its three protagonists, deftly characterized without resort to cliché.

The Picture

RKO RADIO PICTURES and The Filmakers Present *The Hitch-Hiker*:

> *"This is the true story of a man and a gun and a car. The gun belonged to the man. The car might have been yours or that young couple across the aisle. What you will see in the next seventy minutes could have happened to you. For the facts are actual."*

The first victims are a young couple, in a convertible showing an Illinois license plate. They are shot and robbed in the dark night, in a wooded grove. The gun man casually leans down and rifles through the young woman's purse which has fallen to the ground. They are left for dead in their car by the gun man. Throughout the film we only see the gun mans boots as he walks away! His image is like an unidentified dream figure in the distance. A head line which proclaims "Couple Found Murdered" with the rage of the highway killer as he moves across America.

A second headline identifies the killer as Emmett Myers:

We transition to another road. Another pick up.
Another faceless murder – this time is a man.

Another murder, another headline: "Nation-Wide Search for Hitch-Hiker Slayer." This time the victim is a lone man, in a sedan and the hitch-hiker gun man takes his car.

Dawn and a similar car merging onto the highway from a
back road.

The camera reveals the occupants are two men in a 1949 Plymouth.
They are on their way to the Chocolate Mountains on the California-
Mexico border on a fishing trip. The driver is Roy Collins, portrayed by
Edmond O'Brien. He is a mechanic and his friend Gilbert Bowen por-
trayed by Frank Lovejoy is a drafts man. They decide to change their
journey and look for a little action in Mexicali, then do some fishing at
San Filipe, Mexico but Bowen is already asleep in the car.

Daylight and who does the film viewer see standing beside this stolen car, now out of gas?

Collins and Bowen misguidedly pick up Emmett Myers, who gets in
the back seat of the car and quickly pulls his gun on them.

"Face front and keep driving, sure I'm Emmett Myers do what I tell you!"

Myers doesn't immediately kill these two men like he has with his
other hostages. Instead he orders them to drive towards Mexico.

"I'm gonna listen to the news," states Myers. He prefers to just sit in
the back seat of the car and hold his gun on Collins and Bowan, while

"I know what you are thinking Collins—you do not have a chance... you can't tell if I'm awake or asleep!"

they drive him through the desert. Meyer monitors his hunt on the news on the car radio.

"This car rides pretty good," he says. *"Think when I get to where I'm going I'll sell it."*

They hit a bump in the road and Myers orders them to stop the car and get out of it! He orders the trunk of the car to be opened. Bowen has the chance to grab a rifle.

Meyers jerks his gun, *"Don't even think about it, you'll never make it."*

Myers then torments and forces Gill to demonstrate his shooting ability by using his rifle to shoot a can off of a rock and then a soda can out of Roy's hand.

Bowen is more resentful than Collin. *"If you are going to kill us, get it over with."*

Myer's is filled with rage and terror. There is nothing good about this man. He is creepy to look at. Myer's paralyzed right eye lid remains open making it difficult for his hostages to know when he is sleeping.

Collins and Bowen think Myers is sleeping so they unwrap their blankets and take a run for it into the darkness. Meyers runs them down with the car. Collins and Bowen are hypnotized by the headlights and surrender to him.

Another campfire scene, Myers demands Bowen to toss his watch over to him. After looking at it, Myers tells them that he had a watch like this once, only he didn't buy it, he robbed a jewelry store to get his watch.

Back on the road, a flat tire, a busted oil pan on the Plymouth, patrolling aircraft, a pursuing Mexican Sheriff but no shoot outs in the rocks. The tension of this film is all in the incredible performances of these three leading men. The divergent actions and reactions between Myers, the crazed hitch-hiker and the passive two hostages is held completely in the demented personality of the hitch-hiker—he is a bad man with a gun but without it he is a weakling.

Myers later decides to reverse identities with Collins by switching clothes. Not only are they a physical match, but a psychological one. He wants to be Collins to help escape the authorities. The original hitch-hiker spree killer Billy Cook took his captured victim Jim Burke's identification and became him.

The picture ends with a long walk on a dark pier with the sound of a crying cat in the background. The film viewer then hears the sound of a boat motor. Suddenly gun shots are fired.

"Break the lock!"

"Tonight I'm going to chance it."

"Nice and deep!"

"What did you do to it?"

Cut the gab!"

"I want to go now!"

Roy Collins calls out, *"I'm not Myers. Do you hear me? I'm not Myers."*

A fight breaks out between Gil Bowen and Meyers—Bowen knocks Myers to the ground and his gun into the water.

Alto! Alto! is yelled out by Mexican Police authorities. The police walk up to Myers.

He is hand cuffed. Meyers spits on the authorities.

Bowen states, *"Do what they tell you Myers—you are through!"*

Another fight, this time between Collins and Myers while Police have a hold of Myers. Collins hits Myers one blow after another before he is stopped by Bowen.

Mexican Police, *"I'm sorry we have to have a full report."*

Ida Lupino recalls, *"I wanted hard hitting scenes in the opening on The Hitch-Hiker with the audience seeing hard packed drama illustrated with facts! An image appears on screen, no this is not the hitch-hiker slayer but the film viewer will think he is. This was used to build suspense. The viewer then sees shadows and the spinning mage of a newspaper which winds down like the wheel of fortune."*

"I kept the victims faceless to enhance fear that the next murder victim could be anybody—even the film viewer watching the film or the person sitting next to them!"

"*This film was criticized for having a weak ending. I wanted realism! The use of Spanish in exchange for English where the Mexican Police are involved was used to sustain realism. Billy Cook was captured by a Police authority just walking up to him and taking away his gun! The ending of The Hitch-Hiker picture has gun shots along with two different fist fights. It is up to the individual film viewer if they feel the ending predictable. I say it is not!*"

Film Restoration

LOUIS ANTONELLI STATED IN AN INTERVIEW, "In December 1992 as Ida's 75th birthday was approaching, I got the idea to reintroduce *The Hitch-Hiker* to Ida with a new twist; what if we embark on a full restoration of *The Hitch-Hiker*? Make it shine, Ida and be exactly like you always wanted it to be with no compromises? Upon speaking to her about it I was met with the true Lupino fury."

"*Why do you care about that old junk, when no one cares about it? Leave it alone!*"

"This was her sharp reply!

I tried to reason with her, that in truth many people cared. Ida would have none of it!"

"As the weeks progressed into early 1993, Ida changed about the project, in the nature of her good heart, her only concern was that I should in any way not waste my own valuable time on anything to do with one of her 'forgotten films,' when I had fresh pictures of my own to create and exhibit. I assured Ida that my work to bring back *The Hitch-Hiker* would not impede on my own films in any way and it would be real honor to do this project but only with her blessing."

"Ida was deeply touched by this and reluctantly agreed to let me try. Always budget conscious, Ida made me assure her that I would not spend my 'good money' for this 'foolish' but very dear effort of yours."

In 1994, Louis Antonelli began the three year project to restore and reissue the Ida Lupino's Film Noir masterpiece. Antonelli's work on the restoration project was in collaboration with The Roan Group and The

Director Louis Antonelli deep in thought during the restoration of *The Hitch-Hiker* (Michael Prendergast/GRAND CINEMA)

Library of Congress. Louis personally oversaw the film transfer and frame by frame restoration process.

"I never would have imagined in 1976 when I rented a 16mm print of The Hitch-Hiker that years later I would have the honor and blessing from Ida Lupino, herself, to spend literally years of my life working so closely with her original elements of the film to have every single frame sparkle with the original quality it was made with. I felt an urgent sense of responsibility, I could not allow for even the slightest of compromises in this effort. I held firm that Ida Lupino was owed the respect and dignity of a Master Filmmaker and that this particular key work by her must finally be seen exactly as she wanted it to be."

"This was painstaking work on a technical level. There are subtle tonalities within the visual design of The Hitch-Hiker that if not handled with a careful hand would betray the very aspect we were striving to bring back from the murk of Public Domain—the delicate, highly complex Cinemagraphic craftsmanship and artistry that is in The Hitch-Hiker aspects such as the use of degrees of over-exposure in the day time, desert scenes to visually heighten the oppressive heat, which is so key to the hair- trigger tension that primates this film. The night scenes, pools of velvet like densities of black utilized like patchwork of dread shot to shot trapping the characters in their collective fate.

– Louis Antonelli

"I was totally against restoring The Hitch-Hiker. I was very angry, when Louis Antonelli and I first spoke about his project! No one wanted us to make this picture; The Hays Office, The Bureau of Prisons and everyone associated with the film production codes."

"It was Collier Young who really wanted to make this picture and we argued over it. I felt making this picture could ruin our film company if it was not produced carefully—we had specialized in producing films with the subject matter being social events effecting women; women playing the leading roles. Collie won out and I eventually agreed."

"It was a very dark story to write, Collie and I kept changing the title for appeal and believable quality. To make things worse I had to shoot it on a limited budget only $160,000 instead of our usual $200,000. So, I relied heavily on the magnificent geography of the desert landscape and the occasional cut-a way to some police scene for my documentary style of production. Much of this pictures impact was achieved from the fact that it parallels, in many aspects, the Billy Cook man hunt which occupied the nation's headlines so very long ago."

"To even think about restoring The Hitch-Hiker I was against it—I felt that the film viewer of today would think of The Hitch-Hiker as some cult film! It was Louis Antonelli who convinced me of the true importance of this picture and why it should be restored. I knew in my heart that Lou would do a damn fine job restoring it!"

– Ida Lupino

National Film Registry

IN 1988, THE LIBRARY OF CONGRESS passed the National film Preservation Act, and thus established the National Film Preservation Board. The law authorizes the Library of Congress to select and preserve up to 25 films each year to add to the National Film Registry.

The films in the National Film Registry represent a stunning range of American filmmaking, including Hollywood features, documentaries, avant-garde and amateur productions, experimental films, films of regional interest, ethnic, animated and short film subjects—all deserving of recognition, preservation and access by future generations.

As of 2012, there were 600 films selected. The films that are selected must meet two criteria as outlined below:

- They must be culturally, historically, or aesthetically significant
- They must be at least ten years old

The selection takes place after the Librarian of Congress reviews public suggestions and consults with film experts (and the forty members and alternates) of the National Film Preservation Board.

According to Librarian of Congress Dr. James H. Billington, "taken together the films of the National Film Registry represent a stunning range of American filmmaking—including Hollywood features, documentaries, Avant-garde and amateur productions, films of regional interest, ethnic, animated, and short film subjects—all deserving recognition, preservation and access by future generations."

He also observed that "the films we choose are not necessarily either the 'best' American films ever made or the most famous but they are films that continue to have cultural, historical or aesthetic significance and in many cases represent countless other films also deserving of recognition."

For each title named to the Registry, the Library of Congress works to ensure that the film is preserved for all time, either through the Library's massive motion picture preservation program in Culpepper, VA, or through collaborative ventures with other archives, motion picture studios and independent film makers. The Library of Congress contains the largest collection of film and television in the world, from the earliest surviving copyright motion picture to the latest releases.

In 1998, Ida Lupino's classic film *The Hitch-Hiker* was selected for preservation in the National Film Registry as being "culturally, historically and aesthetically significant," due in part to Louis Antonelli's efforts. Sadly, Ida Lupino was not alive at the time to view her restored masterpiece.

Talman as *THE HITCH-HIKER.* CLASSIC PHOTO.

Ida Lupino's informal shooting style of single time and space, omniscient camera angles, lap dissolves and low key action or as Ida called all of this "editing in the camera" has made her a "One Woman New Wave Movement." This has led to the growth of new Ida Lupino fans, young and old alike, who consider *The Hitch-Hiker* her greatest directorial accomplishment.

In December 2012, *Life* magazine re-published their article titled: *"I'm Gonna Live By the Gun and Roam"— Portrait of a Spree Killer* 1951" written by Allan Grant, adding more information with photos never published before. *"Less than a year after he was put to death a movie based on Cook's crime spree and helmed by actress-turned-powerhouse director Ida Lupino was released by Lupino's independent film production company, The Filmakers. The movie is notable not only because it's a better-than-average Noir film but because it's one of the first films ever made in Hollywood that was quite clearly based on a killer whose crimes were still fresh in the minds of the film goers."*

March 21, 2013 marked the 60th anniversary of the premiere of original *The Hitch-Hiker* film. *The Hitch-Hiker* was released to the theatres for audiences on April 29, 1953.

Acknowledgements

I WOULD LIKE TO ACKNOWLEDGE the following companies and individuals for their contributions:

Filmakers
RKO Radio Pictures
The Estate of Ida Lupino
MOVIE The Illustrated History of the Cinema
Life magazine

I wish to thank Paul Green for his research.

Louis Antonelli for his comments, graphics and the use of his rare photo stills for without them this book would not be complete.

And, finally to Ben Ohmart who believed in *The Hitch-Hiker* as a book.

Thank you!

Index

CPSIA information can be obtained
at www.ICGtesting.com
Printed in the USA
BVOW09s2207021117
499361BV00013B/229/P